GOING IT ALONE
WHY JUST WRITING YOUR BOOK IS NOT ENOUGH!

*A PERSONAL GUIDE TO SELF-PUBLISHING
FOR THE SERIOUS WRITER*

GABRIEL FARAGO

This book is brought to you by Bear & King Publishing

Title:	Going It Alone: Why just writing your book is not enough
Sub-title:	A personal guide to self-publishing for the serious writer
Author:	Farago, Gabriel
ISBN:	978-0-9945763-3-0

Cover design and layout by Vivien Valk.

Images from istockphoto.com

Contents

INTRODUCTION

A word of welcome

'Writing my book is not enough? What do you mean?' you demand, a puzzled look clouding your face. 'I just finished mine and it took me years to write. It's DONE! Euphoria; triumph; great sense of achievement. And now you tell me it's NOT ENOUGH?'

Well it isn't. In many ways it's just the beginning and this little book will tell you why.

'And who are you?' you ask, unable to hide your annoyance and your scepticism. This is understandable. I expected something like that. In fact, in your shoes I would ask the very same question. So, let me tell you a little about myself, and what inspired the writing of this little book ...

I'm a self-published author of three thrillers and a collection of short stories—*Letters from the Attic*. My debut novel, *The Empress Holds the Key*, was released in 2013. This was followed by *The Disappearance of Anna Popov* in 2014, and *The Hidden Genes of Professor K* in 2017. These books are available on Amazon, Apple iTunes bookstore, Barnes and Noble and several others, in paperback and as an ebook. May I invite you to have a look at them before we embark on this little journey as you may find it instructive and helpful in following the thoughts and suggestions I would like to share with you.

However, before we do so, I should really introduce myself. Please allow me to share with you my author biography from my website, www.gabrielfarago.com.au:

From Budapest to the Blue Mountains: a writer's journey

As a lawyer with a passion for history and archaeology, Gabriel had to wait for many years before being able to pursue another passion—writing—in earnest. However, his love of books and storytelling started long before that.

'I remember as a young boy reading biographies and history books with a torch under the bed covers,' he recalls, 'and then writing stories about archaeologists and explorers the next day, instead of doing homework. While I regularly got into trouble for this, I believe we can only do well in our endeavours if we are passionate about the things we love; for me, writing has become a passion.'

Born in Budapest, Gabriel grew up in post-War Europe and, after fleeing Hungary with his parents during the Revolution in 1956, he went to school in Austria before arriving in Australia as a teenager. This allowed him to become multi-lingual and feel 'at home' in different countries and among diverse cultures. Shaped by a long legal career and experiences spanning several decades and continents, his is a mature voice that speaks in many tongues.

Gabriel holds degrees in literature and law, speaks several languages and takes research and authenticity very seriously. Inquisitive by nature, he studied Egyptology and learned to read the hieroglyphs. He travels extensively and visits all of the locations mentioned in his books.

'I try to weave fact and fiction into a seamless storyline,' he explains. 'By blurring the boundaries between the two, the reader is never quite sure where one ends, and the other begins. This is, of course, quite deliberate as it creates the illusion of authenticity and reality in a work that is pure fiction. A successful work of fiction is a balancing act: reality must rub shoulders with imagination in a way that is both entertaining and plausible.'

Gabriel lives in the Blue Mountains in Australia just outside Sydney, surrounded by a World Heritage National Park.

'The beauty and solitude of this unique environment,' he points out, 'give me inspiration and the energy to weave my thoughts and ideas into stories which, I sincerely hope, will in turn entertain and inspire my readers.'

So, that's me; in a nutshell. I can see you have a question: *You want to know why I wrote this little book*. The answer is surprisingly simple: many of you asked for it. After I published *The Empress Holds the Key* and it became apparent that I had done it all by myself by 'going it alone,' many of my social media friends wanted to know how it had been done. I was literally bombarded with emails and enquiries on my website, Facebook page and social media generally. At first I thought that I could respond by writing a few blogs about it. However, it soon became clear that this approach wouldn't be enough to do the subject matter justice. So, I began writing this little book instead, while my self-publishing journey was still clearly on my mind. This was my inspiration.

Like you, I spent many years writing my first novel, and when I finally finished it—and began to think 'what next?'—the real challenge began. Actually, it was more like a rollercoaster with many tricky moments and rough turns where you had to hold on tight to make sure you didn't fall off!

This is a literary adventure story. It is the story of how I had to fight my way through the treacherous, ever-changing publishing jungle, the ups and many downs, the highs and countless lows of that remarkable journey. As you can imagine, I've learnt a lot along the way and would like to share some of it with you. Hopefully, this will leave you with a few little polished gems you can use to light up that often quite dark and hidden path, and make the journey more meaningful and enjoyable.

A brief word about self-publishing

The entire publishing landscape has changed—dramatically—and is still changing as you read this. The changes have been staggering, and self-publishing has become a viable, respected alternative to yesterday's 'traditional' publishing.

The unwarranted stigma that once applied to publishing your own work—the *vanity press* of old—has long gone, and not only unknown 'first-timers' are striking out, but many well-established, best-selling authors are now actively looking at self-publishing as an attractive alternative to being 'locked into' a publishing contract where the publisher makes most of the decisions, has most of the say, and keeps most of the money.

Let's have a closer look.

Would you rather be the master of your own destiny, have complete control over your work and how it is presented, promoted, marketed and sold, and keep most of the money generated by it? Or are you prepared to surrender your independence, abdicate from decision-making, hand over the lion's share of the money earned by your hard work in return for the publisher 'doing it all' on your behalf? And perhaps most infuriating of all, would you rather have your work judged by the market, or are you prepared to let the publisher have the final word about the quality and merit of your work, and decide *whether or not it should be published at all?*

Your call.

A word of caution

Self-publishing isn't for everyone, and may not suit you. It's by no means an easy road to travel and requires a considerable amount of hard work, risk-taking, determination, grit, resources and learning many new and often unfamiliar skills.

What I've endeavoured to show you in Part I is a complete overview of all the components of a professionally published book, and more. I've tried to address all the questions, elements and features a mainstream publishing house would consider before releasing a book. It is therefore intended *for the serious writer who is prepared to back himself, and wants to compete on a professional level with established publishing houses.* If this is not what you have in mind, then this little book is not for you.

Part II goes much further, and deals with the all-important subject of building an author profile, marketing and promotion.

Ah … I know what you're thinking! You would rather keep on writing—which is of course what you love doing most—and leave all this boring, confusing stuff to an established, 'traditional' publisher. 'Let him worry about it!' I hear you say, nodding sagely, 'it's all too hard.' You would rather be part of a well-known publishing house, and enjoy the security and prestige offered by a publishing contract. So be it. If the opportunity presents itself, that is. But please be clear about what you are giving up in return. That's all. In the real world, there's no reward without effort, and everything has its price, and 'security' and 'prestige' can be very fickle and often illusory. Please try to remember that.

However, I hasten to add that there is absolutely nothing wrong with taking the 'traditional' publishing route, as long as you know what is involved, and what that means. What I am trying to show you here is an alternative which some of you may find attractive, because it allows you to stay in control, publish your book, and let the market decide how good it really is. If that's what you want, then please stay with me and read on.

PART I: CLIMBING 'MOUNT PUBLISH': Developing your book for release

Let's begin … Climbing that mountain

Your masterpiece is finished, you've approached countless publishing houses and submitted your manuscript for consideration. One after another, the crushing rejection letters keep rolling in. Routine two-liners one and all with no reasons or feedback given. Your spirits sink. Then finally, a well-known publisher decides to have a closer look at it. 'At last!' you think, spirits soaring. However, the publisher procrastinates for months, demands countless changes and gives you the run-around—slowly extinguishing your spark of optimism—and finally rejects your manuscript without an explanation. Catastrophe! You've wasted a year! 'Where to from here?' you ask timidly, despondently.

Sound familiar?

Once you dust yourself off and pick up the pieces, you begin to face the obvious question: 'What now?'

Well, I was there. I know what it feels like and, like you, I stood up, looked around and began to consider my options. I can still remember that watershed moment; most vividly.

What's green and stands in the corner? Usually, it's a naughty frog, but not that time. On that occasion it was me who was green with envy. Envy? What envy? I was looking at successful, self-published authors who had managed to go it alone without the involvement of traditional publishers. They had obviously found a way to publish their books and were enjoying considerable recognition and success. I wanted to be like them, but how? I was determined to find out how they had done it. Come, let me show you what I've learnt along the way.

The good news first: It *can* be done!

Forgive me for stating the obvious which applies to every writer: You stand or fall, you'll be judged, acclaimed or condemned, ridiculed or admired by one thing, and one thing alone: *the quality of your work.* In the end, there's nowhere to hide. This may sound tedious, but it is critically important to understand this at the very beginning, because it has a bearing on everything we'll talk about. Every little detail counts here—and there's a lot to take in and to master—from editing and proofreading to cover design, blurb and book production, to name just a few. And once you've mastered all this, you'll have to start thinking about your website, marketing and promotion, author profile, platform and social media …

Is that you I can see heading for the door? Stop! It isn't as daunting as it may appear right now. Just keep reading and, hopefully, it will begin to make sense and become easier to get your head around. It did so for me.

I know, it's quite a mountain you have to climb here, so let's give it a name. How about *Mount Publish?* But once you start and put one foot in front of the other, it's surprising how quickly you can rise above the clouds and glimpse the blue sky. And once you are up there, well, you can almost see forever.

However, as every experienced mountaineer knows, not only do you need the right gear and equipment, success or failure often depends on meticulous preparation and sound advice. And there's one more important thing you need: *a guide.* Come, let me be your guide. Together we can do this!

The basecamp: polish that manuscript

Make sure you create the best possible manuscript you are capable of, because anything less isn't going to work. And to do this properly and professionally, you will need help and resources.

'Help? What are you talking about?' you ask, unable to hide your annoyance. 'I'm the author, it's my book, I'm the one who's written it. I've devoted years to this project, countless hours—no, days, if not weeks—researching, and now you tell me *I need help*? My work will speak for itself. I don't need any help; thank you.'

You do—trust me! This brings me to ...

TEAM MEMBER I: The editor

TIP: You need a competent, professional editor.

Virtually all successful books on the market have been professionally edited. Without an editor, you might as well pack up now and walk away.

'But ...' you interrupt.

No buts! It doesn't matter how talented you are, how original your ideas, how meticulously you've researched your subject, or how beautifully you write, you will *need* an editor! And to find one you can trust and respect, who understands you and you can work with will, without doubt, be one of the most important decisions you'll have to make if you are serious about becoming a successful, published author.

'If what you tell me is true, how do I find such a person?'

Later. For now, it's enough for you to understand that the right editor can make the difference between success and failure, between fame and oblivion.

TEAM MEMBER II: The proofreader

TIP: You need a competent, professional proofreader.

'All right; so I need an editor. Is that it?'

No, it isn't. Before you can even think about publishing your book, you'll have to have it proofread. You need a *professional* proofreader.

Can you imagine anything more annoying than opening a book you've just bought and finding typos, sloppy punctuation, or confusing, ill-positioned paragraphs? What does that tell you about the book and its author? Incompetence perhaps? Exactly! Your annoyance will override everything and you will not get into the book at all! It has failed before it's even had a chance to engage you. Pesky little errors will not only diminish your work, but undermine your credibility as a serious author. Now, what does a proofreader do? *A proofreader makes sure this doesn't happen to you.*

'But I'm very good at spelling, my grammar and command of language are excellent, and I've engaged a professional editor as you've suggested. Surely, between us, we can do all of this.'

No, you can't.

'Why not? Give me one good reason.'

Both of you are *too close* to the manuscript. You no longer see things clearly and objectively. You need a fresh approach and a fresh pair of eyes. In short, you need someone who comes to the table focusing on one thing alone, without distraction, preconceived ideas or bias, and without having read the manuscript countless times before. You will be amazed what a proofreader will find and pick up. It's a humbling experience which will send icy shudders tingling down your spine!

You see, a traditional publisher would have taken care of these things. But since you've decided to go it alone and become a self-published author, you have to rise to the task and do it all yourself. I must warn you, the learning curve is very steep. It will require discipline and resolve, patience and perseverance, and most important of all, dedication and resources. In short, you'll have to be prepared to spend not only your time, but also some of your money, in getting the basics done properly. You'll have to become an *authorpreneur* like me. If you are not willing to do all this, then self-publishing may not be for you. You cannot expect to create something of value for nothing and without effort! We reap what we sow.

Do I really need to hire an editor and a proofreader?

Before self-publishing your manuscript, it is essential to ensure it is well written, engaging and, of course, free of spelling, grammatical, and punctuation errors. Editing and proofreading is something that many writers believe they can achieve themselves, but the reality is no-one is that good at reading their work objectively and spotting their own errors. Innocuous mistakes missed the first time are highly likely to be missed the second and subsequent times.

Another common mistake writers make is to give their work to family members, friends or colleagues. Unless this person is a qualified editor and/or proofreader, they will also miss errors and, as they know you personally, they may also find it hard to be completely objective (and honest) when reading and assessing the quality of your manuscript.

It has long been acknowledged that self-editing or asking for the help of people you know will not give you the same result as having your manuscript professionally edited. A professional editor has the training and experience to find structural flaws (e.g. in the plot, sub-plots, characters or continuity), and to correct syntactical, grammatical, and typographical errors.

Another misconception is that 'proofreading' will perfect any structural issues with your work, fix all the grammatical issues, and improve your writing. That is not proofreading, it is editing. Editing covers a broad range of skills. More often than not, a manuscript—particularly one written by an inexperienced writer—requires much more than proofreading; it may require a structural or developmental edit and a significant amount of copyediting.

To summarise

Manuscript assessment: If you have just completed a manuscript and are unsure what level of editing it needs, it's wise to have a professional editor cast a critical eye over your work and write up a report outlining the strengths and weaknesses of the work, areas for further development and so forth. This is usually more economical than hiring an editor prematurely to carry out the editing levels listed below. An editor will be your first 'objective beta reader'. The benefit is they have the skills and expertise to pinpoint what works, what doesn't, and what's missing.

Structural/developmental editing: Sometimes also called 'substantive' editing. This involves checking the structure, content, language (including the correct version of English), formatting, style and presentation of your work is acceptable. Remember, you can visualise every character and every scene; you know what is going to happen to whom and when; you know the beginning, the middle and . . . The End. It's not like that for your readers. Keeping the readership in mind, this stage of editing sometimes requires rewriting and usually involves considerable consultation with the writer.

Copyediting: This level of editing checks all the grammar, spelling, as well as ensuring consistency and accuracy throughout the piece. Usually a manuscript is copyedited two or three times (each edit is known as a 'pass').

Proofreading: A final check of a manuscript pre-publication, this usually occurs once the manuscript has been typeset or uploaded into e-book format and involves checking that all elements are included and in the proper order (including front and back matter), that all copyediting amendments have been inserted, that the house or other style has been followed consistently, and that no spelling or punctuation corrections remain.

Note: Some self-publishing/indie-publishing businesses provide proofreading services. If not, you should hire a professional proofreader to ensure your manuscript is perfect before it is published. The editor you hired may or may not offer a proofreading service and some editors don't like to proofread work they have edited, as their eyes are no longer completely fresh or objective to the text and they can miss small things. If you are producing print copies of your book, remember that errors cannot be fixed once it's gone to print!

To conclude, a professional editor and proofreader will ADD VALUE to your writing, resulting in a manuscript that is polished and error free. This can have a huge impact on the success of your self-published book. Readers are more likely to enjoy a well written book; they are also more likely to write good reviews and recommend your book to people they know, and they will purchase other books that you write if they enjoy your stories and style of writing.

How do I find a good editor and afford their services?

Start saving! Apart from working out how much you'll need to cover publishing and marketing expenses for your book, you should also begin putting some money aside for an editor's services while you are in the writing process (or even before). It's wise to get quotes from several editors once your first draft is completed, to get an idea of cost based on the word count and calibre of your writing. Most editors will request an upfront deposit of about 50%. A word of warning: If you think you can find a great editor on FIVERR at $5 per hour or have a friend/relative edit it for free, that's your prerogative, but you probably won't be happy with the outcome.

Be patient. Editors are a diverse bunch and many specialise in certain types of editing and/or specific genres. Take the time to contact several editors and get their feedback/sample edits. It's crucial to find an editor you feel comfortable working and communicating with. If you've written a sci-fi novel, for example, try to select editors who work on this genre. Editors often detail their specialties on their websites or social media profiles (e.g. LinkedIn, Twitter, or a professional Facebook page). You can also visit the websites of writers' associations (e.g., The NSW Writers' Centre, http://www.nswwc.org.au), or your local or national professional editing organisations (e.g. Society of Editors (NSW) Inc., http://www.editorsnsw.com), which have directories listing professional editing/proofreading services.

Maximising the value of your editor's services

Now that you've found your perfect editor and have squirrelled away the money to pay their fee, here are some tips on how to ensure you get the most from their service, and the best outcome for your writing:

Language matters! It's important you are clear from the outset which version of English is the best to use taking into consideration the context, the setting, main readership etc. Once you've decided what version of English you wish to use, make sure you are consistent. Your editor will see which version of English you have used – and if you have mixed up versions he or she will ask you to clarify whether you want it in US English, Australian English, or another version of English.

Spacing also matters. Use double line spacing (or at least 1.5). It's beneficial for you to write using bigger line spacing as you're more likely to spot errors yourself and fix them before handing it to your editor.

Them's the breaks! On long documents, it can be time consuming running the macros to fix this (particularly when there are no breaks at all and the editor has to search for unformatted/unstyled chapter numbers or headings).

Learn how to indent. Again, your editor can run a macro to replace spaces at the beginning of each paragraph instead of an indent or tab, but she'd rather spend her time (and your money) focussed on your writing. Learn how to indent paragraphs and insert page breaks. It's not hard but if you're unsure, use the Help function or ask someone to show you (anyone from Gen Y or Z should do).

Use free grammar/spell-checking tools. Run a spell/grammar check in the correct version of English. Word's spell/grammar check is by no means perfect. You do need to check each error it picks up carefully, and ignore any that are incorrect or unnecessary. Still, it's useful for obvious typos and will catch simple grammatical errors quite adequately. Your editor will pick up everything else, of course!

Given that price is one of the major factors in deciding whether to hire an editor, it seems to make sense to get value for your money by ensuring they spend their time editing your work to be the best it can be, rather than on simple 'housekeeping' jobs that can be done by you. If you are on a tight budget, make the most of your editor's time by tidying up your manuscript or document beforehand.

When you see the significant improvements to your manuscript once it's been professionally edited, you can congratulate yourself on money well spent. Better still, you've begun a relationship with a trusted editor who understands your writing voice and style, and can help you with future projects.

An experienced editor and a hawk-eyed proofreader will, without doubt, be the two most important members of you team. Without them, climbing Mount Publish may end in disaster. Why? Because you stand or fall, you'll be judged, acclaimed or condemned, ridiculed or admired by one thing, and one thing alone: *the quality of your work*; remember?

That's why Sally Asnicar, of FULL PROOFREADING SERVICES,

Web: www.fullproofreading.com.au

has become an essential part of my self-publishing journey.

If I haven't scared you away and you understand that all of this is absolutely essential if you are serious about being a successful self-publisher, then please stay with me and read on.

Title, Cover, Blurb: Your three best friends when they are on your side, or your worst enemies if you've offended or neglected them

You've carefully worked your way through the manuscript, you've engaged an excellent editor and a sharp-eyed proofreader, forged a good working relationship with both and listened to advice. You are pleased. Things are going well, and the manuscript is beginning to look really good.

You are amazed by how much you've learned from your editor, and what a difference professional input from that direction has made. However, you are a little embarrassed and surprised by how many errors and grammar-glitches the proofreader has discovered. Surprised? Don't be. This is normal. The only mistake would have been not to rectify the errors and release the manuscript half-baked. Well, that's not going to happen to you, is it? No embarrassment here.

So, what's next? Look at it this way, you've climbed the first ridge leading up the mountain. You are by no means out of the woods, but still deep inside the forest. Apart from professionally polishing and finessing your manuscript and getting it into shape, the next three tasks you'll have to tackle will, without doubt, have the greatest impact on your book. The viability of your entire project may well depend on them! What are they?

The title of your book, the cover, and the blurb on the back. The importance of these critical elements cannot be stressed enough. Get it right, and you will step out of the woods into the sunshine and see the path leading to the summit in front of you. Get it wrong, and you may well be staring into the abyss of oblivion and failure. So please, pay careful attention.

First impressions are important

All this has to do with *presentation*; the presentation of *your* book. Remember the last time you received a beautiful present wrapped in lovely paper with colourful ribbons and a striking bow—tied with flair—on top? Remember how you felt when you first set eyes on it? When you first touched it? Excitement? Anticipation? Joy? Perhaps all three? Admit it, the wrapping was as important and as memorable as the present inside it! It is the same with books. Miss the moment of first engagement, and you've missed the most important opportunity to hook potential readers. They may never look at your book again. Opportunity lost. You cannot allow this to happen, and to make sure it doesn't, you have to get your book presentation right. Let's start with the all-important book title.

The title

What's in a name? Well, once you think about it, everything, really. Correct. The title of your book is your first opportunity to *speak* to your potential readers, to communicate with them. Do I have to say more? If you fail here, you've lost them. Forever. Your book title must captivate, engage, intrigue, create anticipation, excitement, entice them to find out more, be memorable and, most important of all, *it has to say something poignant about the book*. That's a tall order, I know, and it's very difficult to get it right.

'Hold on,' I hear you say, curling up your nose, 'all this *in a title?* You are joking; surely.'

No; I'm not. I'm deadly serious.

'Well, where do you start?'

'There are a number of tried and tested techniques you can follow. Here, I'll show you the one that worked for me. I had to come up with a title for a 600-page thriller that did all the things I mentioned before: captivate, engage, create anticipation, excitement and be easily recalled—remember? And be true to the book!'

Reluctantly, you nod.

Little gem:

Here's one of the little gems I want to leave with you: *the title of your book is often buried in the text—waiting—and all you have to do is find it*. If you can do that, you are on your way!

In my case, it was a telling phrase in the book, *The Empress Holds the Key*. I must confess that this wasn't the first or only title under consideration. It's almost impossible to get it right straight away. You must live with a title for a while and discuss it with your editor and your friends. Use them as sounding-boards. It may take some time, but in the end you'll know when it's right. You will *feel* it. After all, no one knows your book as well as you do.

Review moment:

All right, you now have a smashing title for your book. You are pleased with it, it ticks all the boxes, your editor has approved it and your friends have given it the thumbs up. You are ready for your next important challenge:

The cover

Who said you don't judge a book by its cover? Whoever it was got it wrong—we all do it, believe me! So, after the book title, the cover of your book is the next most important contact point between you and your potential readers.

Remember browsing in your favourite bookstore on a Sunday afternoon? What did you notice first? Admit it: *the covers*! Well, nothing has changed. In fact, today, with ebooks and electronic 'browsing', the cover is more important than ever. Please pay attention because you have to absolutely get this right if you want to give your book a good start in literary life.

TEAM MEMBER III: The cover designer

TIP: Turn to a professional.

I would like you to keep repeating this sentence, because it is that important. *Never, ever make your own cover!*

'Why not? I have a good idea of what I want and I have a good program on my PC which should do the job easily. After all, I've designed my daughter's birthday party invitation and last year's Christmas card. Everybody loved it! I'll have a go!'

Please don't! Designing a book cover that works is an art and requires years of experience. Therefore, this is another area where you should be prepared to spend some money and engage professional help. After the editor, the cover designer is the next most important professional you need if you are serious about self-publishing.

'Why is the cover that important?'

Once again, this is all about that critical moment of *first engagement* we spoke of earlier: first impressions and presentation—remember? The cover is the most important visual contact between your book and its potential readers. It should be an attractive invitation to come closer, read the title, the blurb at the back, and have a look inside. If it can't do that, you've failed and missed that all-important 'hook' moment. There are no second chances here, and that is particularly so with internet browsing and looking at ebooks.

Browsing is perhaps the wrong term here. Readers browse in book stores, but not on the net. They *skim!* It is very important to keep this in mind and appreciate the difference because it will have a bearing on many things we'll talk about later.

'What's the difference?' I hear you ask.

The main difference between the two is time. The time taken with the activity in question, in this case searching for a book.

Browsing is a slow, leisurely way of looking at things. You take your time, you read titles, blurbs, author bios, perhaps even a page or two of the book. Skimming, on the other hand, is like speed-dating with books, and time is of the essence here where fleeting glimpses and first impressions are the decision makers. So, something must catch your eye, capture your attention and make you slow down to have a closer look. We are talking seconds here. That's where the cover comes into play. Are you with me so far?

'How can a cover do all that?'

Oh, it can—believe me. I'm sure you've done it many times yourself. Better still, let's give it a go right now. Go to Amazon.com and type, say, 'historical thrillers' into the search box. You are not searching for a particular author, but books in that genre. See what happens? You are instantly bombarded with information—pages of it. And what does that information consist of? It's mainly *visual,* right? Pictures. Countless little book covers the size of a postage stamp.

Now, take the next step with me. Which one will you stop at, click on and investigate further and, more importantly, why? It's the picture, the cover that draws you in, right? Perhaps closely followed by the title. Something has connected with you and attracted your attention and it only took a split second. If you could only find out what it was and apply this to your book cover, you'd be on a winner. Well, you can, but you'll need the help of a professional designer to get there.

In some way, the cover must be like the title: it must engage, captivate, create interest and entice you to pause and find out more, and most importantly, *it must be relevant*. In short, it must somehow capture the spirit of the book just like the title, only in a different way. Think of the title and the cover as a team—they have to work together.

As I said before, to do this successfully is an art, as many different elements come into play and must fit perfectly. Colour is of course a very important factor. Colour can create mood, atmosphere, anticipation. It can signal danger, tension, violence, disaster and of course much, much more. And all this before we have introduced any design concepts, shapes, pictures or words. It's complex, subtle and appeals to the senses and the subconscious. Complicated? Yes, it is.

Review moment:
You've engaged an experienced book cover designer, provided a detailed brief which included a précis of your book and a few sample chapters, if not the whole manuscript.

The next step is critically important. You have to ensure your designer *connects* with your book. To do all the things we spoke of earlier, your designer needs to understand and get the feeling of your work. This is all about communicating and capturing the spirit of your book. This cannot happen if the designer doesn't know the book, or has only a cursory understanding of it. Shortcuts won't do here.

Please remember you are in the driver's seat: *you are the client giving instructions*. So, don't be reticent or shy, be proactive. Tell the designer what you're visualising and what you expect. The more detail and guidance you can provide, the better the end result will be. Designing a book cover that works is a collaboration between the author and the designer.

If you leave it all to the designer, it will be the designer's cover, not yours. It's a bit like engaging an architect to draw up the plans for your new home. If you don't tell him how many bedrooms you want, where the garage should be, what sort of style you like etc, it will end up being the architect's home, not yours.

Once again, please keep in mind no one knows your book as well as you do. Ergo, no one is better placed to provide ideas and suggestions, guidance and inspiration for how the cover should look, and what it should convey, other than you. Tell the designer all about your ideas and expectations and I'm sure that with a first draft followed by a couple of rounds of feedback and changes, he or she will come up with a design that works, and one you are happy with. Designers will expect this and respect you for it. After all, it is *your* cover.

Please bear with me for a moment and allow me to illustrate by sharing with you the matters I discussed with my designer when we worked on the book cover for *The Empress Holds the Key*.

To begin with, here is what it looks like:

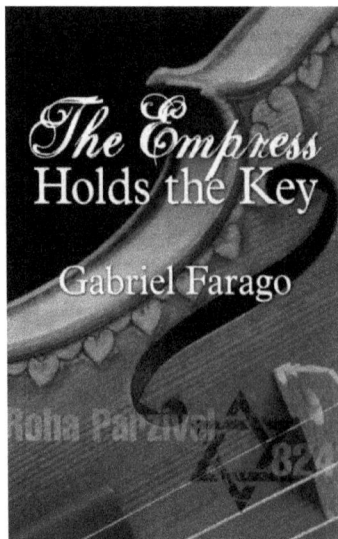

To make this exercise meaningful, we have to understand the type of book we are dealing with here. *The Empress Holds the Key* is a 600 page, multi-layered mystery action thriller for the thinking reader, with a complex storyline, lots of historical material, many exotic locations and fascinating characters. That's your market. So, how do you convey all this in an interesting, eye-catching cover that is pleasing to look at, engaging, and which sends an accurate signal about the content of the book? Not easy, is it?

After a great deal of hand-wringing, soul searching and deliberation, we decided to use the image of a violin as our central theme. Not just any violin, but a genuine Stradivarius with a name. We needed an instrument with character and soul. This was, in my view, a warranted and clever choice, bearing in mind that a violin plays a prominent part in the book.

When you open the book, you will notice that the cover image reaches right across the spine and extends to the back. In fact, when you open the book and put it face down on the table, you can almost see the entire instrument spread out in front of you.

Remember, there's nothing arbitrary about any of this. Everything has a specific purpose and function, and all of it is designed to *engage*.

For me, for this book, the colour tones had to be warm and inviting and pleasing to the eye. Raising questions, three faded images—a Star of David, the words *Roha* and *Parzival*, and a set of numbers—float out of the violin's f-hole to add mystery and intrigue to the look and feel of the cover.

Needless to say, all of this is quite deliberate. The images floating out of the violin were chosen due to their relevance to the storyline—each plays a part in moving the story forward, and each steps forward into the limelight from a place of history in the story. Of course, the cover doesn't reveal their actual significance—it's the book which does that job—but designing a cover with intrigue like this should encourage you to at least consider finding out more about the book with a view to buying it!

When the reader has finished reading the book, puts it down and looks at the cover, he will now see it in an entirely different light. Suddenly, the images have meaning and make perfect sense. The title, too, will speak to him in a completely different way. All the questions have been answered. This is all part of the overall experience of reading this book. It should be memorable and lasting, and most important of all, it should entice the reader to want to read more of *your* work! That is what a carefully designed cover can, and should, do for you.

Since publishing *The Empress Hold the Key*, I have written two more novels, namely, *The Disappearance of Anna Popov,* and *The Hidden Genes of Professor K.* By way of further illustration, I have included the covers of both books. Here they are:

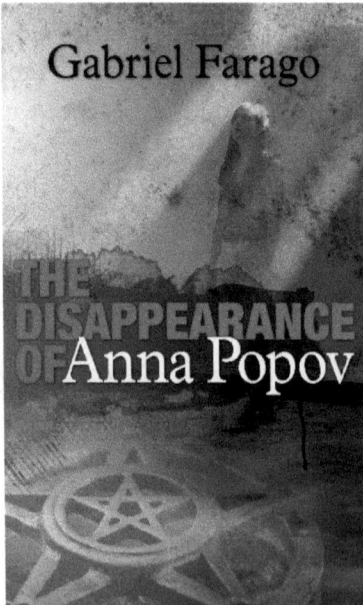

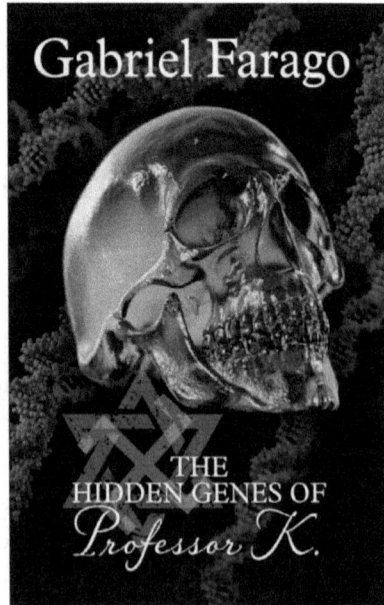

Review moment:

After several attempts, much soul-searching and a few tense moments with your designer, an excellent cover has been created for your book. You are delighted. You now have a title that works, and a cover to complement it. You are almost ready to go. However, one more hurdle remains: the blurb, or description.

The blurb

To avoid any misunderstanding or confusion, let's make sure we all understand exactly what a blurb is, and what it does. The blurb is a brief book description on the back cover of the book. It is often accompanied by an author photo and a few words about the author. However, please bear in mind that all of this is still part of the overall cover design.

You've caught the 'browsing eye' or, more accurately, the 'skimming glance' of your potential reader with your cover, you have created interest with your title and planted curiosity, and now it's up to the blurb to get him over the line. If you fail to engage here, there will be no sale; you've lost your would-be reader. Forever. He has already moved on. So, the blurb has to do the trick.

The best way to illustrate how this works is to show you one and analyse it. I would like to do this by using the blurb on the back cover of *The Empress Holds the Key*.

Let's begin with your brief: You have to come up with a concise description of your book—in this case a complex, multi-layered thriller of more than 600 pages—make it interesting, accurate and true to the text, create interest and arouse curiosity without giving too much away, sketch one or two main characters, outline some of the plot, refer to a few key locations and do all of this in say, no more than three paragraphs (about 200 words). Got it?

I can tell you, this is really difficult. As we said before, no one knows your book better than you do, and it therefore stands to reason that it is you who is best equipped to draft a blurb that works. Still, to come up with something that does all of the above is infuriatingly hard. Nevertheless, it must be done, and it must be done well. You can ask your editor to help you here, but in the end it's going to be up to you. It will take some time, a fair amount of exasperation and numerous drafts, so please be patient and persevere. This is not the place for compromises or second best. It's just too important!

This is the blurb on the back cover of *The Empress Holds the Key*:

> Journalist Jack Rogan knows a great story when he finds one. A charred old photograph found in the ruins of a cottage hints at dark secrets and unwittingly reignites an ancient and deadly quest for a holy relic mysteriously erased from the pages of history.
>
> Police officer Jana Gonski in pursuit of a suspected Nazi war criminal joins forces with Rogan, barrister and amateur archaeologist Marcus Carrington QC, and celebrated composer Benjamin Krakowski. Together they uncover a murky web of intrigue and greed, hoards of Nazi gold and hidden Swiss bank accounts. All implicate wealthy banker Sir Eric Newman. When Newman goes on trial, unexpected clues are discovered pointing the way to a mystery that has haunted the Catholic Church for centuries.
>
> On a dangerous journey to find the relic, Rogan and his companions trace links back as far as the reign of Akhenaten, the heretic pharaoh of ancient Egypt, and King Solomon and the Queen of Sheba. What is this dark secret guarded by the Knights Templar, and so feared by the Vatican? Will religious fanatics foil this quest which could destroy the very foundations of their Church and challenge Christianity itself?

Now, please answer the following questions: Did you find the blurb engaging and did it 'draw you in'? Has it sparked your interest and ignited curiosity? Did it give you enough of a 'flavour' of the plot, the characters and the setting to make it all appear interesting and exciting? In short, has it tempted you to buy this book, or at least to find out more about the author and his work?

Next to the blurb is an author photo, and a few words about the author which may help:

> Gabriel Farago is an Australian author, lawyer and novelist with a passion for history and archaeology. Gabriel holds degrees in literature and law, speaks several languages, and has studied Egyptology. He travels extensively and visits all of the locations mentioned in his books. Gabriel lives with his wife in the Blue Mountains near Sydney.

This short biographical note is designed to provide a brief glimpse of the author, his background and 'credibility' as a serious writer. It's only a sketch, but should complement the blurb and further engage the 'skimming reader' and help to get him 'over the line'. It should introduce the author, and show that a real person of interest stands behind the book. Bear in mind you have only seconds to do this, so every word counts!

By way of further illustration, I thought that having a look at the blubs of my other two novels might be helpful. Here they are:

The Disappearance of Anna Popov

When Jack Rogan, celebrated author and journalist, stumbles on a mysterious clue pointing to the tragic disappearance of two girls from Alice Springs, he can't resist investigating.

Rogan is joined by friends: Rebecca Armstrong, his New York literary agent, Andrew Simpson, a retired Aboriginal police officer and Cassandra, an enigmatic psychic as he follows the trail of the missing girls into the remote Dreamtime-wilderness of outback Australia.

Soon, past the point of no return, they enter a dark web of superstition and are drawn into the upside-down-world of an outlaw bikie gang where the ruler is an evil master, outcasts are heroes, and cruelty and violence is admired and rewarded.

Cassandra, though, has a secret agenda of her own. Using her occult powers to avenge an old, deep wrong, she sets the scene for an epic showdown where the stakes are high and the loser faces death and oblivion.

Will Rogan succeed? Will a desperate mother's prayers be answered? Will a lost daughter be found? Or will the forces of evil crush all their hopes and dreams?

The Hidden Genes of Professor K

World-renowned scientist, Professor K, knows he's close to a ground-breaking discovery. He also knows he's dying. With his last breath he anoints Dr Alexandra Delacroix as his successor and pleads with her to carry on his work. Delacroix unwittingly enters a dangerous world of unbridled ambition and greed that threatens to destroy her. Desperate and alone, she turns to celebrated author and journalist Jack Rogan.

Alistair Macbeth, self-made billionaire and enigmatic founder of Blackburn Pharmaceuticals, has a murky past. He knows he must secure Professor K's discovery for his empire, or perish.

Powerful and ruthless, he will stop at nothing to achieve his dark and deep desires.

Meanwhile, when the parents of famous rock star, Isis, are brutally murdered, Jack Rogan is asked to investigate.

On a perilous journey of discovery which takes them around the globe, Jack and Lola Rodriguez—Isis' resourceful PA—join forces with Jana Gonski, a former police officer; Dr Bettany Rosen, a tireless campaigner for the destitute and forgotten; and Tristan, a gifted boy with psychic powers. Together, they expose a complex web of fiercely guarded secrets and heinous crimes of the past that can ruin them all and change history.

Will Rogan succeed? Will the dreams of a visionary scientist with the power to change the future of medicine fall into the wrong hands, or will his genius benefit mankind and prevent untold misery and suffering for generations to come?

Little gem:

Reading is very subjective. So is taste. What may be considered a gripping plot and fascinating characters by one, may be viewed as pedestrian and boring by another. A sentence is not a formula—diverse outcomes are possible despite the words being the same. There is no certainty here; everything is subjective. Because a work of fiction appeals to the imagination, to feelings, senses, emotions, and so on, it will have a different effect on every reader. Therefore, please keep in mind that *you cannot, and will not, appeal to everyone*. Nor should you try. Be true to yourself as a writer, trust your instincts, and do not be distracted by what others *may* think, and thus compromise the integrity of your work.

'Is that it? Are we ready to go?' you ask, chomping at the bit.

Not quite, I'm afraid.

'Why not? What's left to be done?'

Quite a bit. You have to design the layout of the text. In short, how your book will appear and be presented *between the covers*. And as you will see shortly, there's more to it than first meets the eye. You're making all the decisions here—remember? We'll bundle it all together and call it *Between the Covers*.

'Between the covers'—Book layout and design

All right; let's take stock. You now have a professionally edited and proofread manuscript, a fabulous cover and engaging blurb with author photo and short bio. It all looks great; you are excited. However, one more vitally important task remains: designing how your book will look *inside* the cover and this involves a number of important, quite technical decisions. Let's begin with the font.

The font—type and size

There are literally dozens of fonts to choose from. First and foremost the font must be pleasing to the eye and easy to read. Font size is important, too. So, how do you find a font that works for you and your book? I'll tell you. But before I do, here's a little story I would like to share with you.

It all happened at university a long time ago. We were a group of four inseparable friends studying law—jokingly referred to as the Four Musketeers. Always together; always late for lectures; always broke. All four of us had part-time jobs in the same restaurant close to the university. We didn't earn much, but we got by and shared everything. Most of the time we had little or no money and were hanging out for Thursday. Thursday was payday.

Then something happened which I have never forgotten. Suddenly, Midge—his real name was Michael, but we called him Midge because he was very short—began to pay for everything. When we went to dinner in our favourite little Italian restaurant, which we did every Tuesday because the meals were half price, he insisted on paying. When we went to the pub after work on Saturday, he shouted drinks all night. Suddenly, Midge was flush, with wads of cash in his pocket. He didn't come from a wealthy family and his job, just like mine, didn't pay much. Not surprisingly, it wasn't long before we confronted him about this. I was conscripted to interrogate Midge after one of our Tuesday half-price dinners.

'All right, mate, where's it coming from?' I asked, pointing to the wad of bank notes in Midge's hand as he was once again preparing to pay for our dinner.

'From an idea,' he replied, a cheeky grin on his face.

'Would you care to elaborate?' I asked.

'No, I'll do better than that. I'll show you.'

'Oh? How exactly?'

'We're going to the races.'

'The races? When?'

'Tomorrow.'

This was entirely out of character. Quietly spoken, a little shy and very reserved with a phenomenal memory that often left us gobsmacked, Midge was the last person we would have expected to be interested in horseracing.

He was, without question, the smartest of us all. I'd never seen him go to the library; he hardly took any notes during lectures and regularly skipped tutorials. When we crammed for exams, he went to the beach. Yet he got distinctions in most subjects, and seemingly without effort. Whichever way you looked at it, Midge and gambling of any kind just didn't go together.

Wednesday was race day at Randwick. I was the only one in our group who was free that morning to go with him to the racecourse.

'What exactly are we doing here?' I asked, following Midge through the throng of excited punters to the bookmakers at the front. He seemed to know his way around, which surprised me.

'Stay close and watch.' For a while Midge just stood there, keeping an eye on the bookies. Then suddenly, he made a move. He walked up to one of the bookmakers, pulled out a wad of notes and put $50 on a horse.

'Are you crazy?' I asked. 'Did I just see you put fifty bucks on a bloody horse?' This was quite a lot of money at the time.

'You did.'

'And what do you know about this nag? About form, racing, odds?' I demanded.

'Absolutely nothing,' replied Midge, grinning.

'Jesus, Midge, you're out of you mind!'

'Far from it. Come, let's watch the race.'

Half an hour later Midge's horse won, and he collected $500. I was speechless.

'Okay, Midge, *how*?'

'Do you see those blokes over there?' he replied, pointing to a group of well-dressed, middle-aged men in suits and hats standing next to the bookies.

'Who are they?'

'Big punters. I mean *big*. Syndicates.'

'So?'

'When I see them make a move, I do the same. I get into the line behind them, listen, and then place a bet on the same horse they've decided to back. They put a thousand bucks on that horse. That was good enough for me. I put on my fifty. You've seen the result.' The logic behind all this was as simple as it was compelling, but obviously not without risk.

'Does it work every time?'

'No, not every time. But overall, I'm in front—by miles!'

'Are you suggesting the race was rigged?'

'Don't know. Doesn't really matter. If these guys are prepared to risk a thousand bucks, I'm prepared to risk fifty. I call it the piggyback principle. You piggyback on what the big boys know, and what they do. It's that simple.'

Midge told me later that he had learnt this from his granddad who used to take him to the races every week when he was little. His grandfather had supported his family with this simple little trick during the Depression.

The lesson? *Watch, learn and emulate.* After this, Midge became *Punter Midge.* He's a Supreme Court judge now, and we still have dinner together every couple of months or so. However, I don't think he's going to the races any more. How do I know? He stopped paying for dinner, that's why.

Whilst I'm certainly not suggesting that horseracing and book design have something in common, the message is clear: watch what the big boys are doing, and learn from their experience and success. In short, emulate. And that is precisely what I did here. You can rest assured that a lot of thought, hard work and resources have gone into the design and presentation of a successfully published mainstream book by publishers and a raft of experienced professionals. This is how it worked for me:

First, I had a close look at my successful competitors. I chose three books I particularly liked, and carefully analysed their layout and design. In particular, I looked for the font and size that appealed to me most.

'How do you know which font was used?' you interrupt.

Well, very often the font and the font size are actually noted on the inside cover, and all you have to do is find the reference! Once I saw my manuscript in the chosen font and was happy with the way it worked, I used that font for my book.

I adopted the same approach for the other book design criteria we are examining here. So, let's move on to the next decision you have to make: the layout of your page.

Page layout

After the font and size, the layout of your pages is the most important book design decision you have to consider. What is involved here is the all-important line spacing, paragraph indents, margins and positioning the page numbers. These are all *separate* decisions which will impact on the overall feel and appearance of the individual pages, and therefore the book generally.

To get this right, you've again looked at your successfully published competitors, selected the page layout you particularly liked and applied it to your text. A little experimentation here comes in useful, as you may not wish to slavishly follow all aspects of one particular page layout. You may decide to follow, say, the line spacing of one of the books you liked, and the margins and the page number positioning of another. See what works for you, discuss it with your editor first, and then decide. Follow your instincts: your critical eye will tell you when it's right. That's exactly what I did, and this approach worked well for me.

Allow me to illustrate this. Please open one of my books at random and look at the double page in front of you. At the top of the left hand page you have the author name at the centre, and at the top of the right hand page you have the book title. The page numbers are centred at the bottom of the pages; even numbers on the left, odd numbers on the right. The margins and indents have been carefully chosen to balance the page. Once again, the page must be pleasing to the eye and easy to read. Cram in too much and the page appears crowded and too busy; space things too far apart and your lines and paragraphs get lost. It's all about balance.

You'll no doubt be pleased to hear that we've reached the final decision you'll have to make here: choosing the best paper colour for the pages of your book.

Paper colour

'Is that important?' you ask. Yes, it is. Very. Needless to say, this will only apply to the print version and not to ebooks. Usually, the choice is between plain white and cream. Most novels have cream pages which are warmer, softer on the eye and easier to read. I chose cream for that reason, and I'm sure you'll end up doing the same.

'At last! My book is ready to go,' you announce excitedly, feeling pleased with yourself.

Unfortunately, I have to disappoint you—no, it isn't! Not yet.

'Why not? We've done everything you suggested. My book is now complete, you tell me. What else do I have to do?' you ask impatiently, unable to hide your annoyance.

Quite a lot, I'm afraid, and you should have started doing it all well before you finished writing your book and began to address all the things we spoke of earlier.

You look genuinely puzzled. 'What are you talking about?'

Preparing the way for publication.

'I don't follow.'

No, I didn't think you would. That's why writing your book is not enough. Here, let me explain why that is so.

PART II: RIPPLES IN THE POND: Marketing and promotion

Your website—the hub of the wheel

All roads lead to Rome, or in this case, to your website. Look at your website as the main contact point between you, the author, and the outside world. It's the sign above your shop, the ad in the paper, the entry in the phonebook, the name on your office door all wrapped into one and much, much more. I'm therefore stating the obvious when I say to you that it's of vital importance to make a good impression right from the start.

Consider your website as your cyber-persona: it IS you, what you stand for and what you represent. More often than not, it's the first serious contact point between you and your potential readers. It is what the cyber-world *sees* and how it learns about you, how it perceives you and how it judges you and what you stand for. It is an extraordinary opportunity to *introduce* yourself and your work, and it is absolutely crucial to get this right from the very start. Once again, you only have seconds to do this, and if you fail, your visitors will move on and rarely return for another look if you don't engage them. There are no second chances.

TEAM MEMBER IV: The website designer

TIP: You need a professional to design your website.

Once again, this is all about first impressions and presentation. If you want to be a professional writer, you must present yourself as one. You don't go to an important job interview dressed in the t-shirt and baggy shorts you wear in the garden or to the beach, do you?

Designing a website that is captivating, classy, has style, originality and draws you in, holds your attention and persuades you to linger and find out more, is an art; believe me. It would be naive to suggest that an amateur having a go using free material and instructions available on the net can do all this and get it right. You don't remove your own appendix by following instructions gleaned from a free manual you've just downloaded from the net, do you? So, don't make the big mistake of trying to do this yourself. You only get one bite at this juicy cherry—don't choke on it. Once your website has been launched, *it's out there* for all to see, good or bad. You just cannot afford to get this wrong if you want to succeed. Reputations often take a lifetime to build, but can be destroyed in the blink of an eye.

Let's recap. You need a competent and experienced website designer. This doesn't have to cost an arm and a leg, as our first website doesn't have to have all the whistles and bells, but it must look good, and do the job. You can start with baby steps, but they must point in the right direction! You can always expand your site and add more features later when you have a better idea of what works for you, what you need and what you can afford.

'Where do I start? How do I know what I need?' you ask, looking a little exasperated.

Simple. Do you remember the piggyback principle we spoke of earlier? Well, that's what you do. You surf the net and visit websites of well-known, published authors in your genre until you find a few you like. Narrow them down, and note the features you've found impressive and incorporate them into your own site. Then, when the time comes to instruct your own designer, you will already be well-informed and able to tell them, and *show* them, what you want. It's no different really from telling your book cover designer what you have in mind.

An experienced designer will then advise and guide you, and pull it all together. However, please remember that it is *your* site, and you are once again in the driver's seat here. The designer will expect input from you, so if you want to be taken seriously and end up with a site that reflects who you are and what you stand for, you need to guide your designer clearly.

There is one more important point to keep in mind here. All your marketing efforts, especially social media which we'll discuss shortly, will be designed to drive traffic to your website. If the site fails, it was all for nothing, but if you get it right, you are well on your way to creating an interesting author profile, and a sound platform for launching and promoting your work.

Once again, please allow me to illustrate this by taking you to my own website. Needless to say, I do this for a good reason. Because I obviously know it intimately and have been part of its development and creation from the very beginning, I will, hopefully, be able to point you in the right direction and assist you in avoiding the more obvious, and often costly and disastrous, pitfalls you will encounter along the way.

May I therefore invite you to visit my website at www.gabrielfarago.com.au. As you'll see, a lot of design work and thought have gone into creating this multi-faceted site. Please turn up the sound end enjoy the journey.

I would now like to take you through the site in some detail, explain its various components and functions, and show you what they are designed to do, and how.

As you'll see, the site is divided into five separate pages, or parts, if you like: **Home, Biography, My Books**, **Blog** and **Contact**.

Home page

To begin with, I had to decide on a concept and a theme. Once again, first impressions are important. I wanted to create something that would entice visitors to my site to enter my world, the world of the writer, but with a specific link to my first book—*The Empress Holds the Key*. I thought an engaging way to achieve this would be to take visitors on a journey of discovery.

To do this effectively, my designer and I decided to use a short video with 'image-signals' and sound effects. I like to think of this as communicating through objects, settings and scenes to create a certain mood and a particular image.

For the sake of authenticity, the entire video was taken at my home in the Blue Mountains where I do most of my writing, and all the objects and artefacts used belong to me. All objects have been carefully chosen and have specific relevance to the book and the inspiration behind it.

I wanted the mood to be mysterious, and the overall look to be old-worldly and interesting, but most important of all, I wanted to engage the visitor from the very beginning by igniting a certain curiosity. For the site to work effectively, it must be capable of persuading the visitor to stay with you in order to find out more, rather than lose interest, abandon the search and move straight to the next one. Needless to say, that's critically important when skimming has replaced browsing, and split-second timing is of the essence. That's where the experience and artistic talent of your web designer comes into play.

The main tools here are originality communicated through engaging content, in this case both visual and audible. In short, you have to *offer something of interest*, just as we've tried to do with the book title, cover and blurb. The objectives are the same, and so is the brief.

You will note that the **Home** page concludes with an invitation to *Solve the Mystery*. This is done by inviting the visitor to click as indicated, and once they've done that, they're taken straight to **My Books**. Why? The reason your visitor has decided to enter your site in the first place was most likely the fact that you are a writer and they want to find out more about you and your books. So, give them what they came for, quickly and easily. By making this step 'interactive', you have once again created interest and curiosity.

My Books page

Your visitor is still with you, and has given you the opportunity to showcase your work. So, you must do just that. This can be done in a number of creative ways, but a short, engaging summary of your book is essential here. Consider this as a 'blurb on steroids'.

Remember you are selling your book here. Therefore, the same principles apply to this exercise as to the blurb we discussed earlier, except that this can and should be an expanded, fleshed-out version. Needless to say, to include a photo of the book cover is a must, and if you've done a good job with the cover, it will work well here, too. As you can see, everything is interrelated, and quite intentionally so. Let's not forget, you are building a *brand*. Also, if your book or books have already been published, you must tell the visitor where they can buy them.

You will note that the **My Books** section opens with a clear and easy to follow link to where the book can be purchased. By clicking on, say, Kindle, the visitor will be taken straight to Amazon where they can instantly purchase and download the book. Simple. By making this step easy and user-friendly, you are considerably increasing your chances of a sale.

You're in luck. Your visitor is hooked and wants to find out more about you and your work. To keep them interested, you must once again offer something of interest and value. But what? You will note that the **My Books** section concludes with an invitation to follow me into my attic where my letters are waiting. Intrigued? I hope so, because that's the idea. By clicking as required, the visitor will be taken to my **Blog** which I've decided to call *Letters from the Attic.*

Blog roll

We'll deal with blogs in more detail later. However, a few introductory words about blogs and blogging are warranted here.

In my view, blogs are tremendously important. Why? Because they are a wonderful opportunity to showcase your writing, provide short, punchy samples of your work, introduce yourself as a serious writer and talk about your books and what inspires your writing. For that reason I've decided to integrate blogs into my website from the very beginning rather than feature them in a different place later on.

If this is done well, you'll be able to entice your visitors to come again, follow you, and perhaps refer others to your site. Please remember that your website is the hub of the cyber-wheel. It is the main contact point between you and the outside world. We mustn't lose sight of this, as all the social media strategies we'll talk about later are designed to drive traffic towards your website. If the destination is disappointing, your visitors will regret the journey and will almost certainly abandon it and not come back. So, it pays to channel a lot of effort into this. It's a no-brainer.

Finally, I would now like to turn to the last remaining page on our website; the author **Biography**. As you can see, I've left this to last. This was of course quite intentional.

Once the visitor has entered your site and you've enticed them to stay with you and look at your books and read your blogs, it's time to introduce yourself and let them meet the author.

Biography page

The best way to do this is through a short, I repeat *short*, but interesting biography. Once again, this should be written in an engaging and entertaining style, preferable peppered with photographs illustrating the text.

Everyone loves snapshots from the past, and there's no better way to engage your visitor than inserting a few interesting ones right here. This gives you the opportunity not only to *tell*, but also to *show* something about yourself. Things become personal. As we shall see later, pictures are tremendously important here. They are a wonderful and most effective tool I use constantly, not only on my website and in my blogs, but especially in my social media posts. I like photography, and take most of the photos myself. This gives my pictures a personal perspective that has served me well. If you cannot do all this yourself, you can source pictures from the net, or engage others to take them for you. But whatever happens, you must use pictures because they are so effective.

By way of illustration, please allow me to refer you once again to the biography I've used on my website. In fact, you've already read it; it's set out in full in the Introduction! However, if you visit my website at www.gabrielfarago.com.au and turn to the **Biography** page, you'll see how we've utilised photos to make it more interesting and engaging.

Contact page

It is vital that you provide an easy to follow and user-friendly contact mechanism to enable visitors to your site to get in touch with you. Each email you receive should be answered promptly and courteously, as each contact you receive here is valuable and forms part of a database you can use going forward to promote your work. Please have a look at the **Contact** page on my website and see how it has been structured. The page speaks for itself.

Blogging

We've touched briefly on blogging before, but it's now time to address this all important topic in more detail and in the context of social media, marketing and promotion.

As you'll soon discover, you have to put a lot of work into your blogs. I certainly do. Most of them are carefully crafted short stories with a specific purpose and theme. Blogs must be very well written. More often than not, they are the point of first contact between you and a prospective reader. In short, they are the first opportunity for you to showcase your writing and present it to the outside world. And most important of all, this will happen long before you publish your first book. You are trying to build a reputation while also creating an environment in which to launch your book. Therefore, great care must be taken to produce the best writing and storytelling you can muster because *you are on show!*

Sloppy writing, careless little mistakes, typos and formatting glitches are unforgivable and must be avoided at all cost. The reason for this is obvious: you are introducing yourself as a serious writer. You want your readers to take notice and follow you. This can only be done if you impress them with your work. If your blogs aren't worth reading, do you think anyone will be interested in your *books?* You know the answer.

Your blogs must therefore *offer something* to the reader. If you want visitors to return, you must entice them to do so, and you can only do this successfully if you have impressed them with your writing and originality, entertained them with your stories, ignited curiosity and then left them wanting to read more. That's a tall order. Just ask yourself this question: would you persevere reading a badly written, boring blog and then come back for more? That just isn't going to happen. You've wiped yourself off the radar without even a blip. There's only one way to make sure this doesn't happen to you: write excellent, memorable blog posts that shine and leave a lasting impression.

The best blogs I've come across are no longer than, say, 700 or 800 words. The really good ones are self-contained short stories, and as every serious writer knows, short stories are notoriously difficult to write. However, there are many entertaining blogging styles, and you will have to find one that suits you, that you are comfortable with and good at. Using photographs is an excellent way to make the text interesting and engaging. For that reason, I've tried to use photographs whenever possible.

The best way to demonstrate this is through examples. My posts fall into two separate categories: biographical, and what I call the 'journey of the book' posts. Allow me to explain.

'Biographical' blog posts

Permit me to take you to one of my short, 'biographical' blogs—**The Major and the photograph in the window**—and you can see for yourself.

The Major and the photograph in the window

Ask any serious storyteller if he can remember the first story he told in public. I'm sure he can; most vividly. I certainly remember mine.

It happened at school in Austria many years ago. I must have been about ten or eleven at the time. Before sending us home for the day, our teacher told us that we would all have to tell a little story to the class the next day. Instead of being intimidated by this, I was actually very excited. I had been telling stories to my grandmother and my two great aunts who were living with us, for years. I remember when they got tired of listening to me, I used to tell stories to Lumpi, our dachshund, who was usually asleep by the fire. So, the most difficult thing for me was not to think of a story I could tell in class, but which one to choose. I settled on the one about the Major and the photograph; one of my favourites.

When the teacher called us—one by one—to the blackboard the next day, I could hardly wait for my turn. This is the story I told the class:

'It happened in Prague on a warm Sunday morning in the spring of 1904. The dashing young officer—a major in the Austro-Hungarian army—had just arrived by train from Budapest. Looking very dapper in his uniform as he crossed the Charles Bridge, he was on his way up to the castle to meet a friend.

Not only the young women promenading on the bridge, but even the haughty matrons hurrying to church turned their heads as he walked past. When he left the bridge and entered the Little Quarter, something caught his eye in the shop window of a well-known photographer. The major stopped, lit a cigarette, and looked at the photograph displayed on an easel in the window. It was a portrait of a young woman sitting on a chaise lounge. *She looks like a Greek goddess*, he thought, fascinated by the striking woman in the photograph. The officer stood there for a long while, oblivious of the throng of the passers by giving him curious looks.

The major returned to the studio on Monday morning and asked to speak to the photographer who had taken the picture he had so admired the day before.

"Can you tell me who that young woman is in the photograph over there?" he asked, pointing to the picture in the window. At first, the photographer was evasive, and didn't want to provide any information. The major insisted. In those days, one didn't refuse a request made by a senior officer in the Austro-Hungarian army. Rolling his eyes, the photographer relented with a shrug, reached under the counter, and opened his appointment book.

"The young lady is the daughter of a prominent doctor," he said. "The photograph was taken in the family home here in Prague a month ago."

"May I have a name and an address, please?" asked the officer.

"The family lives near Bertramka …"

"The villa where Mozart composed the overture to Don Giovanni a few hours before its premiere?" interrupted the major.

"That's the one. The doctor lives next door."

"I know where it is."

The major called on the doctor the next day, introduced himself and described the curious incident with the photograph in the window.

"I can't quite explain it, but something about the young lady has affected me deeply …" he told the doctor. "Is she here? Would it be possible to meet her?"

"Yes," said the doctor, smiling, "come." He took the major to an open window overlooking a beautiful garden at the back of the house, and pointed to a young woman of about 18, sitting on a bench with a book in her lap. Looking up, she waved to her father. When her eyes turned to the handsome stranger in the uniform standing next to him, her heart missed a beat.

Three months later, the major and the young
woman were married. That's how my grandfather
met my grandmother.'

Let's take a closer look at this blog post. First question: did you enjoy it? You did? Good. Second question: did you learn something about the author? Yes again? Excellent, because that was the idea behind it. I wanted to show the reader a little bit about myself, my background and my life, but in an indirect and entertaining way. I look at these posts as little windows giving you a glimpse of the past, but you must be subtle doing this. Beating your own drum too loudly is never a good idea and quite often falls on deaf ears. This is most important to remember if you want to build an author profile that is interesting and engaging and leaves a lasting impression without sounding like self-promotion. And finally, and perhaps most importantly, did you like the style of writing? If we can answer all the three questions in the affirmative, we've hit our target.

'Journey of the book' blog posts

Now, let us briefly examine one of these blog posts. You will note that a quite different approach is needed here. You are introducing the subject matter of the book, albeit indirectly. This must be done in a subtle, entertaining manner. You are *guiding* the reader, not *telling* him. It is always a mistake to underestimate your readers and overshoot the mark by being too forceful, patronising or direct. Don't forget your writing is on show here. Let it shine and do the heavy lifting. If you cannot reach your readers through your blog, create interest in your writing and the subject matter, then why would they want to read your book? Simple; let's have a look and see if it works:

The Officer and the Monk

'Buried deep down in one of my grandfather's old army trunks—covered in cobwebs and almost hidden behind wooden beams in the back of the attic—I made a surprising discovery. I found his journals, a little mouldy and difficult to read, but otherwise intact. The tiny, spidery handwriting, the faded ink, and the badly creased pages made them almost illegible. Not surprisingly, I pushed them aside. They were of little interest to a 10 year old boy. It would be many years before I opened them again and began to delve into my grandfather's hidden world.

However, at the very bottom of the trunk, I found something else which turned out to be far more interesting to me at the time. At first, I didn't pay any attention to the rusty tin, the size of a shoebox. But when I opened it, I discovered something extraordinary; postcards, dozens of them, neatly tied together with string.

All the postcards were addressed to my grandfather and had been sent from Egypt by someone called Lucius. I spent the next couple of hours sitting on the dusty floor looking at the pictures—mainly drawings—of temple ruins, colossal statutes of strange gods and boats with triangular sails crossing the Nile. There were also pictures of camels, palm trees, hippos, crocodiles and turbaned men in long flowing robes. Images of a different, distant, exotic place—Egypt. These postcards were my first contact with an ancient culture that has fascinated me ever since.

After the excitement of my new discovery had died down a little, I carried my new find down to the kitchen to show my great aunts—both of them fabulous cooks—who lived with us at the time. The kitchen was their domain and they ruled it with iron-fisted military precision. I was responsible for the firewood and lighting the fire in the huge stove every morning at first light.

I put the tin on the kitchen table, opened it, and said: 'Look what I found in grandpa's trunk.' Aunt Frieda came over and looked inside the tin.

'You found his postcards,' she said, smiling. 'From Egypt. I had no idea he had kept them.'

'Who is Lucius?' I said, holding up one of the postcards and pointing to the signature on the back.

'Father Lucius was your grandfather's closest friend,' said Aunt Rosa. She opened the oven door and looked inside. There are certain things you never forget. The mouth-watering aroma of freshly baked bread that filled our kitchen every time Aunt Rosa baked bread was one of them. 'He was a Franciscan monk,' she said. 'He lived in Egypt for many years. Your grandfather visited him there once. They spent a few months together exploring the monuments of ancient Egypt. Come to think of it, your grandfather brought back many exotic things from that trip,' said Aunt Frieda. 'Perhaps they too are in those trunks?'

I ran up the stairs back to the attic and began to rummage through the other trunks. At first I found only books; many of them about Egypt. But then I found the real treasure: strange artefacts. Scarabs, small stone statues and many etchings and lithographs.

It soon became apparent that my grandfather had been quite a scholar with some surprising interests, especially for a career soldier serving in the Austro–Hungarian Army. When I eventually opened his journals again many years later, most of what I read made no sense. The concepts and ideas, the many references and quotes simply just went over my head. The breakthrough came when I discovered that a particular set of quotes was in fact an extract from a book in his library right here in the attic! It was like opening a window to let in sunshine and fresh air. After that, everything began to fall into place.

The book in question was a history of a fascinating order of notorious warrior-monks, The Knights Templar. As I was soon to discover, the Templars and their secrets was one of the three main topics addressed in the journals. The other two dealt with the pharaoh Akhenaten—the heretic king of Ancient Egypt—and a French priest who lived in the 19th century.

At first, these topics appeared unrelated. However, as I began to delve deeper into the journals, I discovered that this was far from so. What brought them all together was another extraordinary discovery. One of the leather-bound journals at the bottom of the trunk which I assumed belonged to my grandfather, didn't belong to him at all. It was the diary of his best friend, Father Lucius!

The two learned friends had collaborated for years to unravel an extraordinary mystery. This mystery involved the Templars, the pharaoh Akhenaten and a French priest. This fascinating story inspired me to write *The Empress Holds the Key* which will be published in November.

However, to prepare the way, I will tell you more about the Templars and Akhenaten, and especially the enigmatic Abbe Sauniere and his secrets. In addition, I will release a free ebook called *Letters from the Attic* which will throw further light on the journey of the book and, hopefully, pique your interest to read it once it is published.'

Let's have a closer look at this blog post and analyse its components. In essence, the reader is taken to the very beginning of the journey, the very source, the inspiration behind the book. Make no mistake, this is a very powerful tool. You are providing a glimpse into the private world of ideas and inspiration that have motivated the writing of your book. This creates a very personal connection with your readers, an intimacy which rarely happens in traditional publishing. I believe this is a tremendous opportunity to engage your readers and keep them with you. You are, quite literally, taking them on a journey. You are also taking them into your confidence. They are invited to follow you behind the stage, into the dressing room. You show them the costumes and the props, introduce them to the actors and let them read part of the script. In short, you are preparing them for the performance to come. This is precisely what I've tried to do through my blog posts during the ten months leading up to publication, and I'm pleased to tell you, it worked. Very well, in fact. Why? Let me show you.

You will note that the blog concludes with a brief reference to *Letters from the Attic*. Something new, and I believe quite innovative and unique has been introduced.

What is it? It's a concept, an idea to pique the reader's interest in the journey of the book. How? By giving something away for free, and as we all know, everyone likes something for free, especially if it has some value. I believe *Letters from the Attic* has real value and, judging from my readers' reactions, its effectiveness and popularity in paving the way for the publication of *The Empress Holds the Key*, proves the point.

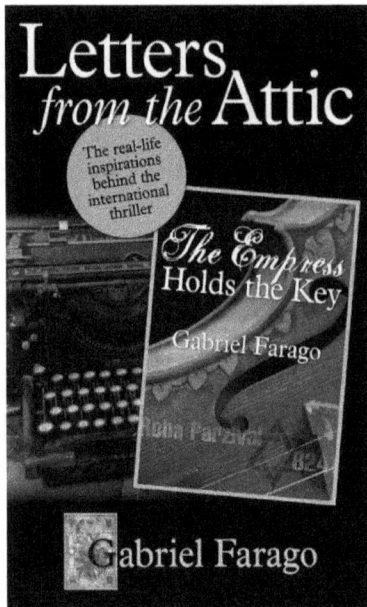

So, what is *Letters from the Attic*? The introduction describes it as: The real-life inspirations behind the international thriller *The Empress Holds the Key*.

It is a compilation of my blogs which were released every Friday during the lead-up to publication and is dedicated to 'all the seekers who strive to understand the past, to help them make sense of the present, and allow them to shape the future'.

The introduction then poses the question:

What goes on in the mind of a thriller writer? Where do authors draw their inspiration from? Becoming a writer doesn't happen in a vacuum. It is a journey in itself that provides the material for the stories, and the rich tapestry of characters and settings that bring those stories so vividly to life.

'This collection of short stories was inspired by my popular blog Letters from the Attic on my website www.gabrielfarago.com.au and provides a glimpse into my world and the creative process that shapes my work. One way or another, all of these stories relate to my new thriller The Empress Holds the Key, and will help you understand the journey of the book, and demystify the arcane craft of creative writing.'

These blogs were all carefully crafted to tell a story, the story of the book. By bundling them all together and releasing them as a free ebook a few weeks prior to publication, *Letters from the Attic* was in fact a book trailer, paving the way for the publication of *The Empress Holds the Key* in December 2013.

'Was it effective?'

Yes, very. To begin with, it was released on Smashwords because I wanted it to be free. Amazon didn't allow this; the minimum download charge was 99 cents. The whole idea behind the release of *Letters from the Attic* was the fact that it didn't cost anything, and could therefore be quickly distributed worldwide to reach as many potential readers as possible. It was a small, personal promotional gift, from author to reader. It was therefore instantly available to anyone interested in the book, and it was free. In fact, it still is, and you can download it right now at: http://www.smashwords.com/books/view/369771.

May I invite you to do so, and have a closer look? I will let *Letters from the Attic* do the talking and you can judge for yourself whether or not I've been able to engage you, and 'pique your interest'. However, please keep in mind that potential readers from as far away as Iceland to Argentina did in fact download *Letters from the Attic* by the hundreds, and by the time I published *The Empress Holds the Key* in December 2013 I had, due to a simple little idea, a ready market waiting for the release of my book.

We must briefly pause here for a moment, and turn to another important point that has a direct bearing on the website, blogging, and our social media strategy which we'll discuss a little later: *timing*.

Timing

I began building my website about a year before I was ready to publish my first book. I began blogging at about the same time and was actively putting my social media strategy in place.

'Wasn't that a little too early?' you interrupt, 'especially if you didn't have a book to work with and to show?' I asked myself the very same question, and until an experienced social media coach explained to me why that had to be so, I was just as sceptical. However, once she took me through the reasons and strategies behind all this, it began to make perfect sense. She called it the *'chicken and the egg principle'*. I can see you frowning. Allow me to explain how it works:

Before you can consider releasing your book, you have to create a platform from which to launch it.

'A platform? What do you mean?'

You can't release a new book into a vacuum. If you do that, you are destined to fail. You are an unknown author without a track record. No one knows you; no one has heard of you. It's a bit like leaving your manuscript on a deserted park bench in winter for someone to find and read.

Before you can even think about stepping out into the challenging world of publishing, you have to create an environment in which you are known. At least a little.

'Create an environment? What do you mean?'

Until a few years ago, this whole idea would have been considered a nonsense; an impossibility. However, with the advent of social media, it can be done. You can build an author profile, create interest in your writing and the book you are about to release *in advance of publication*, so that by the time you are ready to publish your book, you have an audience and a potential market, however small. Look at it as a toehold climbing up the cliff face leading to the summit. Without that toehold, you cannot take that all-important first step, and you will be forever staring longingly at the summit which will remain frustratingly out of reach.

Can you see where this is heading? You have to build that toehold *before* you can step outside and begin to climb. Your website and your blogs are your building blocks, and your social media strategy the mortar that holds it all together. *They are your toehold.* For this to work effectively, you need both, and it all has to fit—perfectly. Is this beginning to make sense? I hope so, because without it, there's no successful self-publishing.

'So, are we done?' you ask.

No; not yet, I'm afraid. Two more critically important items remains. You have to add two more members to your team. You need a *facilitator* specialising in self-publishing, and a social media coach.

'What on earth do you mean?'

Allow me to explain.

TEAM MEMBER V: The 'facilitator'

TIP: Use a competent and experienced 'facilitator'.

Once you've finished your manuscript and it is ready to go, it has to be carefully formatted before it can be uploaded to, say, Amazon, Smashwords and all the other publishing platforms. This is a complex and critically important task. Get it wrong and you'll be forever chasing your tail. You will curse the moment you decided to do it all yourself; trust me.

True, it is possible to do it all yourself, but just like building a website that works, designing a book cover that is engaging, and attending to the all-important editing and proofreading tasks, you need an experienced professional to do it for you. To make mistakes here is just too risky and could easily jeopardise the entire project. To engage a facilitator therefore makes good sense.

'And what exactly does a facilitator do?' you ask. The best way to answer this is to refer you to the website of the one I have used when I began self- publishing, namely, MoshPit Publishing's IndieMosh service, which you can find at **www.indiemosh.com.au**

IndieMosh describes itself as '*a self-publishing facilitator providing editing, proofreading and e-publishing services to Australian indie authors*'. These services are becoming more widely available all the time, and I have no doubt that you'll find a competent service provider in your area who can guide you and assist you in sourcing your team members.

I have used MoshPit Publishing's IndieMosh service in several ways, the most important of which was in the formatting and uploading of my first few manuscripts to make them available on Amazon, the Apple iTunes bookstore, Kobo, Barnes and Noble and several others. You can also use your facilitator to suggest a competent editor and proofreader. In fact, you may find that the facilitator also offers these services.

The lesson here? Do your homework when engaging a facilitator, because you are adding a valuable member to your self-publishing team.

Social media—the pebble in the pond

Do you remember as a child standing on the banks of that mysterious little pond, looking at the still, green water, thinking *what if?* And then what did you do? You picked up that pebble and threw it as far as you could towards the middle of the pond. Remember what happened? I'm sure you do. After that initial little splash, ripples appeared, moving in concentric circles—quite quickly and silently—away from the splash towards the shore until the whole pond was bobbing up and down, and the water was still no more.

Well, social media is just like that. One little splash can make a huge difference and create waves that can reach every corner of your publicity pond. You just need the right pebble, and then the skill and dexterity to throw it into the middle of the pond. As with all things, there's a knack to it.

You're shaking you head. You don't believe me? Alright, just sit right back and let me show you why, and how it can do just that.

There's never been a better time to be a writer than right now, especially for a self-published one. The opportunities are unprecedented and have never been greater. Gone are the days of garages or cellars full of printed copies of your book waiting to be placed in (mostly small, independent) bookstores, hoping to catch the eye of a browsing would-be reader prepared to give an unknown author a go. You have to learn to think BIG. The whole world has become your bookstore. This is no exaggeration, believe me. However, it doesn't happen by itself. It's hard work, lots of it. It's possible, but it's up to you to make it become a reality, and you have to begin well before you start thinking about publishing your book.

'Why?'

I'll tell you why.

You have written a masterpiece. Perhaps *War and Peace*, *Lord of the Rings*, *Gone With the Wind*, or *To Kill a Mockingbird*? If no one gets to read it, it was all for nothing. It will remain on that lonely park bench, forgotten, and soon it will be covered in snow, lost forever. Every author wants his work to be read. That's what this is all about—right?

The thoughts and ideas created in your mind, must reach the hearts and minds of others. How do we do this? We communicate: we transmit our ideas, thoughts and feelings to others. There are a number of ways we humans can do this.

The writer does it through the written word, through language and writing. The written word is one of the supreme achievements of man, and at no other time in human history has it been possible to reach so many, so quickly and with such ease. You are in the right place at the right time! Right now. Here. Today! Please consider this carefully.

Take a moment and think of your work as a popular piece of beautiful music. The melodies are your stories, the notes the words. You are the composer and the conductor, the orchestra is your publicity machine, the musicians are the professionals who helped you produce and publish your book, and the concertgoers are your readers. If your work isn't performed and recorded, no one will hear it and experience its beauty. It will languish in lonely anonymity, forgotten, withering away before it had a chance to blossom and soar. No orchestra, no performance; no performance, no audience. No audience, oblivion. Failure.

So, how do you make sure this doesn't happen to you? You must put your work out there for all to see and to judge. Let the market—your readers—decide if it has value and appeal and not some obscure, anonymous publishing committee with a purely commercial agenda that has little to do with the merit or true potential of your books. You stand or fall by the quality of your work—remember? Nothing else.

'And how do I do all this?' you ask, looking a little frazzled.

You publish of course and then market and promote your work, rigorously, using the marvellous, often quite breathtaking new tools that are now freely available to you. Let's walk into the cyber-store of social media and see what's on offer, shall we?

Social media, a relatively new term, is a catchall. It includes all the obvious big stars such as Facebook, Twitter, LinkedIn and Pinterest, but there are several others, and new ones keep coming with ever-increasing speed to make things even more confusing and difficult to get your head around.

Let me state the obvious here: it is impossible to master them all, become proficient, produce results, and then still have time to write which, after all, is what you are really good at and want to do—right? Social media is a tool, albeit an important one with huge potential, but it's still *only a tool*. You are in control.

Therefore, it's all about choice. You'll have to decide which tool you are most comfortable with, enjoy using, and will serve you best. However, before you can make an informed decision here, you must have a clear understanding of each of the tools, how they operate and how they can help you achieve your goals. It's your decision.

TEAM MEMBER VI: The social media coach

TIP: Social media is here to serve you, not the other way around.

It is terribly important to remember that. Many of you who already use social media for different purposes will know that it can be quite addictive, and take up a tremendous amount of time. Don't let this happen to you. Don't let the tail wag the dog! Social media is not here to *entertain* you, but to *serve* you, and if handled correctly, it can perform wonders. Let's have a closer look:

Social media play a pivotal role in self- publishing, and an experienced social media coach can teach you how to utilise these amazing tools to your best advantage.

Depending on what stage of your self-publishing journey you are on, a social media coach will review your current online presence and provide clarification of how effective your online platforms are, offering guidance, and help you improve your author branding and e-book promotion.

At first, I thought I can do all this easily myself; no problem. However, I soon found out that the complexities involved in addressing this properly, needed the assistance and guidance of an expert. That's when I turned to Lama Jabr of Xana Marketing for help. Lama became my social media coach and marketing adviser, and another valuable member of my team.

Website: http://xanamarketing.com

As things turned out, it was one of the best decisions I made along the way. Why? Here, let me tell you.

It soon became apparent that author branding on social media is an essential aspect of self-publishing. Author branding is a very useful tool. It allows readers to engage with you, find out who you are, what you do and, most importantly, gain more information about your books through an accessible, user-friendly platform.

An experienced social media coach can help you to:

- *Clearly identify your target audience*

- *Create a powerful brand that stands out*

- *Develop a solid e-book marketing strategy so that your book has increasing accessibility*

- *Assist you in creating effective content and maintain this content on all platforms*

- *Reach a wider audience, attract more loyal followers, connect and engage with your target readers*

- *Open more doors for bigger and better opportunities*

- *Gain knowledge and awareness of how to effectively utilize social media tools, monitor, analyse and improve your results*

- *Raise awareness about your book and author branding*

- *Provide training on how to effectively utilise your online presence so you spend more time writing not more time managing your social media platforms.*

Once Lama and I began to address these complex subjects together and I learnt how to access and use social media in the right way, my author profile quickly took shape, and my book sales started to improve; dramatically! I was going in the right direction, and had mastered another challenge thrown at me by Mount Publish.

Facebook

Choices are subjective, and we all make decisions for quite different and often perplexing reasons that are difficult to explain. This is especially so when it comes to dealing with social media. I've given a lot of thought as to how best to tackle this. Please allow me to tell you what has worked best for me.

I've decided to make Facebook the centrepiece of my social media campaign, use it to build an author profile and a following, and prepare the way for the publication of my future books. Because there's only a limited amount of time available to do this without allowing social media to 'take over' and seriously eat into the time you have to devote to being a writer, I've decided against using Twitter as well. After having had a close look at all the options and how they worked, I realised that I couldn't do everything. It came down to a choice. However, I've decided to add LinkedIn and Pinterest to my campaign, but more of the reasons behind this later.

I published *The Empress Holds the Key* in December 2013, and began my social media campaign in earnest during March that year. This is how it all came together:

I was in New Zealand at the time, putting the finishing touches to my book. I had a handful of Facebook friends, no followers and no 'likes' at this stage. I had a careful look at Facebook and how it worked. I liked the concept and began to appreciate its huge potential.

Sitting on the terrace of our house in Queenstown overlooking the mysterious Lake Wakatipu, I began my campaign.

By the time I published my book nine months later, I had 1700 carefully chosen Facebook friends, about 200 loyal followers, and close to 700 'likes' on my Author Page with a growing database of email contacts I could use going forward. These were my 'ripples in the pond,' and it was truly amazing to see what these ripples could do if harnessed correctly.

Let's pause for a moment and consider the numbers. There are many successful authors with a much larger Facebook following than mine was at the time. However, we must not underestimate the true potential of the numbers. This is why:

We can safely assume that each of my Facebook friends has on average at least 100 friends each. Remember, my friends have been carefully chosen, and if they decided to post something about me or my work on their pages, it would have a potential reach of about 170,000 Facebook users. If each one of those 'friends' were to tell, say, three of their friends about my book, this would have a further potential reach of about 510,000. See where this is heading? The numbers are certainly impressive and increase exponentially. However, it all comes down to the *quality* of your contacts, the quality of your posts, your personality and ultimately your book. You stand or fall by the quality of your work, remember? Nothing has changed except for this: *you now have a potential market that can evaluate your work. You are out there!*

All of this has been achieved organically, without any paid advertising. In short, it didn't cost me anything except my time. I firmly believe that was the best way to tackle this by far. However, I hasten to add that it has taken a lot of hard work to get there—albeit very satisfying and enjoyable—and I've learnt a lot along the way. Set out below are a few little social-media gems I would like to share and leave with you. You may find them useful:

1. Treat every one of your Facebook friends as an individual, just as you would in real life.

This is not a numbers game. If you are serious about *connecting* with people, you have to treat them as such. Welcome each of your new friends by sending them a short, personal note. I've tried to do this in an engaging and entertaining way by sending a photo of my grandfather's old typewriter with the following welcome message:

NEW FRIENDS LIKE YOU MAKE IT ALL WORTHWHILE!

Please visit my website at www.gabrielfarago.com.au to learn more, and stay in touch.

Cheers!

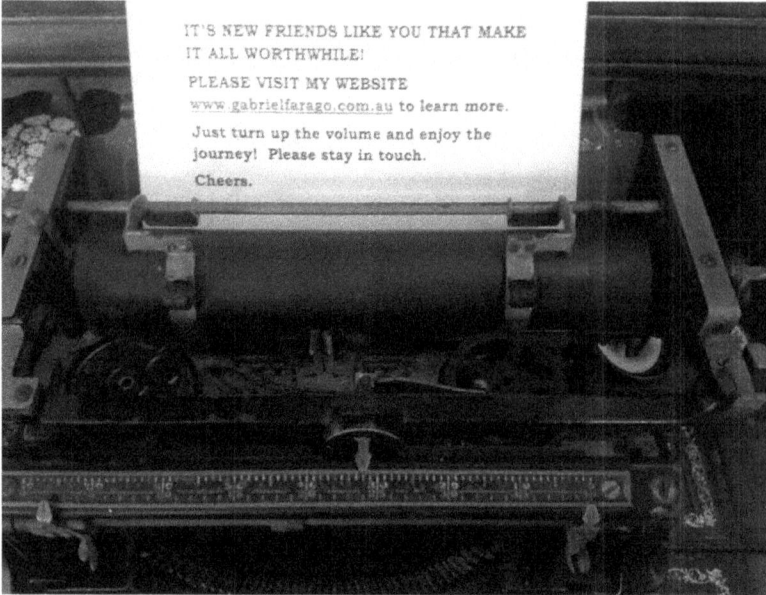

Judging from the reaction and the comments I've received, this has worked remarkably well.

2. If someone asks you to like their page please visit it and, if you genuinely like it, do so.

Every time I liked someone's page, I followed up by sending this message:

YOUR PAGE WAS EASY TO LIKE!

May I invite you to visit mine at
http://www.facebook.com/GabrielFaragoAuthor
and, if you like what you see, return the
compliment?

Do you know what happened? Almost everyone did. That's how you build your 'likes' in a genuine and meaningful way, and create relationships and contacts that last.

3. Visit your page every day, and reply to messages and invitations promptly.

The reason for this is obvious. Not only is it courteous to do so, but it clearly shows that you care and are interested. To reply days or weeks later is often pointless; opportunity lost.

4. Posts are your centrepiece. Make them as interesting as possible, and post something several times a week.

An important way to make posts interesting and engaging is through pictures. The text must be short and punchy and the subject matter original. Wordy posts get lost and are rarely popular. An original photo with one sentence can often create a phenomenal result. Visual engagement is an excellent tool here.

I can sense your exasperation.

'How do I know what works and what doesn't?' you ask. May I once again refer you to our 'piggyback principle'? Have a good look at other Facebook pages and take note of the posts you like. Analyse them. Ask yourself why you liked them. What is it about them that has attracted you? If it has caught your eye, chances are that others, too, have found the post of interest. Then try to apply the same approach to your own posts. It's all trial and error. However, if you persevere, you'll soon get the hang of it and away you go. That's exactly what I did, and it didn't take long for all of it to come together.

'All right; how much time does all this take?' you demand.

I must admit that's a really tricky question. Spend too much time on this and you'll soon get lost without sufficient time to do all the other important tasks you have to attend to here. Do too little, and the campaign flounders and ultimately fails. It's a balancing act without a formula. Unfortunately, I can't give you a precise answer here; you'll have to find your own way I'm afraid. I can only tell you what has worked for me, and why, and explain the balance I've tried to strike in keeping all the important balls in the air.

I spend about one hour each day attending to social media tasks. But please pay attention to the words *each day*—that's the really important message here. You must be consistent and diligent; a little bit every day is the key to this. Miss a few days, and you fall hopelessly behind. Playing catch-up is a recipe for disaster. It doesn't work.

Once again, I think the best way to illustrate this is by example. May I invite you to visit my Facebook author page at http://www.facebook.com/GabrielFaragoAuthor.

To make this exercise meaningful, please go back to the very beginning of the page and have a look at the posts in chronological order. Examine their subject matter, and how they have been structured. This will give you a historic perspective of how the page has developed, how it has grown, and why.

Every post, every reply, every contact you make is important here. These are the building blocks of your marketing campaign. They hold the structure together. You never know how or from where a breakthrough will come. Let me give you an example:

One of my Facebook friends who lives in France and works for a radio station, decided to review *The Empress Holds the Key* on French Radio (23 February, 2014). I had no idea he was going to do this until he posted a reference to it on my Facebook page on 23 February. This is what he had to say:

> 'I have just finished reading that book, and have reviewed it on my weekly program, on French radio. It is a very good book, a true adventure story! Nicely written, no wasted space with boring endless bios to build up the characters. It involves some moral issues, but doesn't labour them, like a lot of writers do. A mystery/thriller is just that, and not an excuse for bodice ripping, or pushing a pet subject disguised as a thriller with a token thriller content. There was only one section, which I found a slight [sic] tedious, involving a court speech: it

could have been shorter. There are one or two edits needed, to tidy up some punctuation etc. but the continuity of the writing and the story is not affected. It is far better than Brown's *Da Vinci Code*, which really speaking isn't that good. Brown's book was hyped up by a good media machine, and quite a number of people I know were very disappointed. Having said that, the film was very good, but then, films don't have the space for the baggage that you find on the printed pages. This book has a good ending, and I was sorry to have to stop reading, when the book finished. I read it in two sittings! My review can be heard on the link on my FB page in this Sunday's program.'

The impact of this review on French Radio was astonishing, to say the least. Suddenly, I had a readership and following in France, and book sales soared. And all of this because of one contact, and one review, albeit, on a popular radio station. Ripples in the pond—remember?

Pulling it all together

Let's pause for a moment, take a step back and have a closer look at where we're at:

You now have an excellent website, and all the essential pages, Home Page, My Books, Blog, Biography and Contact Page are working well together. You've had your site professionally designed because you realised that it is the hub of the cyber-wheel. In fact, it *is* your cyber-persona, your window to the world outside.

You've given careful consideration to blogging and have crafted a series of interesting blogs which you have placed on your website. You understand that blogs are the perfect vehicle to engage visitors and showcase information about yourself and your work. You have decided to extensively use photographs to illustrate the text because you know that pictures are so effective.

At the same time, you have turned your mind to marketing and promotion, and have begun your social media campaign about a year before your book was ready to go. Why? Because you realised that you cannot successfully release your book into a vacuum. As an unknown first-time author, you know you have to create the right environment for your book debut in order to give your book the best chance of success in a highly competitive and unforgiving environment. How? By using social media. You throw the pebble into the pond.

You've walked into the social media store, and have familiarised yourself with what's on offer, and how it all works. You concluded early on that you couldn't master all there was and use everything effectively. You therefore had to make a choice. You've found what works for you, and have begun to focus on, say, Facebook, like I have, and decided to make it the centrepiece of your campaign.

So far so good. You are rapidly adding new friends to your growing Facebook circle, and creating interest in your website by driving 'traffic' to your site.

However, there are a few additional things you can do to add further 'punch' to your campaign. Let's have a look at a couple of obvious ones and examine how they work and what they can do for you.

An article in your local paper

Approach your local paper, make contact with a journalist and tell him or her what you're doing. Suggest an interview.

'Is that likely to happen?' you ask.

I bet you'll be pleasantly surprised. It's actually easier than you may think. Journalists are always on the lookout for interesting stories, especially local ones they can use in regional papers. It's up to you to make yourself and your work relevant. In short, you have to *sell* yourself. If you can do that, you'll land an interview and an article, and the impact of that can be quite extraordinary. A BIG ripple in the pond. This is exactly what happened to me.

I approached our local paper here in the Blue Mountains—the *Blue Mountains Gazette*—made contact with a journalist and told her about myself and what I was doing. An interview followed, culminating in a delightful article that opened many doors. Here, let me show you. This is the article that appeared in our local paper two months after I published the *Empress Holds the Key*:

www.bluemountainsgazette.com.au

Entertainment, the arts and dining

Diverse interests: Leura author Gabriel Farago.

Passion for history has thrilling results

By Jennie Curtin

He was born in Budapest, educated in Austria and moved to Australia when he was 17, so it's hardly surprising that Leura resident Gabriel Farago has a broad range of interests.

Many of these are canvassed in his first novel, *The Empress Holds the Key*, which embraces such subjects as ancient Egypt, King Solomon and the Queen of Sheba, the Knights Templar and a police officer in pursuit of a Nazi war criminal.

Mr Farago has degrees in literature and law and speaks several languages.

A self-confessed "inquisitive" man, he has studied Egyptology and learned to read the hieroglyphs.

He spent 35 years as a lawyer, including some decades at the criminal bar in Sydney, and started work on the book about seven years ago after retiring from full-time legal work.

He describes his novel as "a thriller for the thinking reader" and says his passion for history informs his work.

"I take history as we know it and I say "what if". I ask, what if things had been different? So I weave fact and fiction together.

"By blurring the boundaries between the two, the reader is never quite sure where one ends and the other begins."

But he believes a successful book is a "balancing act: reality must rub shoulders with imagination in a way that is both entertaining and plausible".

The Empress Holds the Key is published by Hazelbrook-based MoshPit Publishing and is available at Megalong Books in Leura, as well as in ebook form from Amazon.

It was launched in December and reaction has already been very positive, Mr Farago said, probably because he had devised a pre-publication marketing campaign using social media to attract a potential audience.

Mr Farago has spent most of the last year blogging on his facebook site about the development of the book and some of the inspiration behind it, including the diaries of his grandfather, an officer in the Austro-Hungarian army.

He is thrilled with the worldwide response to the book, citing emails from Argentina, Finland and Iceland.

Many of them have asked him how he utilised social media so effectively, so he is now working on a self-publishing guide book, subtitled "why just writing your book is not enough", to share the story of how he has used social media to generate knowledge of and interest in his book.

"I call myself an author-preneur," he said. "The traditional publishers used to say, leave your manuscript here.

"They decided who to publish. They became the gatekeepers and were completely in charge.

"For the first time, you can now do it yourself and the market decides on your success."

Approach local bookstores

Because it was likely the article would create quite a bit of interest in our local area, it became obvious that the book had to be accessible and easily available for potential readers to purchase by the time the article appeared in the paper. The internet alone is just not enough here; not everyone is an ebook reader who can and will download your book or an online shopper willing to wait for your book to be shipped. Many prefer the traditional way and want to *see* and *feel* a print copy. So, what to do? Approach your local independent bookstore, introduce yourself as a local author and persuade them to stock your book.

'Is that likely to happen?' you ask.

The answer is *yes,* especially if you tell them that an article in the local paper is imminent and that the bookstore in question is most likely to get a mention. That should remove any reluctance. Needless to say, you must have a copy of your book with you, and you should leave it in the store as a 'teaser'. If you can offer some promotional material as well, you may even get a window display, and that would be quite a coup.

'What kind of promotional material?'

Here, let me show you.

Prepare suitable promotion material

An eye-catching poster is an excellent start and easy to produce. Try to make an impression by being original. If you make it easy for the bookseller and perhaps even offer to help prepare a window display, the more likely they are to go along with your suggestion and give you a go. This is an excellent opportunity to promote yourself and your book in your area, and it's all free.

This is the poster we designed and distributed in key locations; eye-catching and simple.

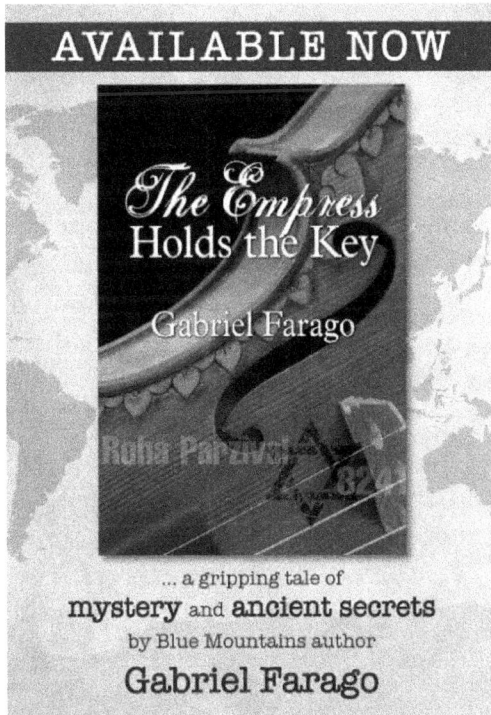

Generally speaking, people are rather fascinated by authors and word spreads quickly, especially in the local community. You may be surprised how much interest a small window display about you and your book can generate and what other doors it can open. Perhaps a brief appearance on local radio or even on TV? You just never know. In fact, these things somehow seem to snowball, developing a momentum all of their own.

After *The Empress Holds the Key* was made available in our local book store in the Blue Mountains just outside Sydney, I was approached by a large, well-known book store in the city with a proposal.

'A *proposal?*'

Yes. Not only was the store going to stock the book, it suggested a book launch to promote it! This was totally unexpected.

Book launch

Admittedly, this may not happen often now, as 'traditional' book launches are becoming quite rare, but if it does, it is a tremendous opportunity to put yourself and your book 'out there'.

Such events are very popular and provide excellent exposure and a splendid photo opportunity and stories for blogs, posts and articles. All grist for your growing publicity mill. Readers love meeting authors and have them sign a copy of their book. This is personal contact at its best and, if the opportunity arises, embrace it. It doesn't come any better.

However, please do remember what we said at the very beginning: you stand or fall, you'll be judged, acclaimed or condemned, ridiculed or admired by one thing, and one thing alone: *the quality of your work*. Nothing has changed.

Finally, just a brief word about something else that may help you promote your book and build your author profile: *talks and seminars*.

Talks, appearances and seminars

With articles appearing in papers and magazines and your reputation as an author spreading, it is quite likely that you will be invited to give talks, participate in college seminars and events such as writers' festivals, appear in libraries to sign copies of you book, and perhaps even be interviewed on TV. Embrace every opportunity and *participate*! Again, this may not suit everyone, but if you can manage it, hold up your hand because it is an excellent vehicle to further enhance your standing and reputation as an author. Do it, but do it well. Prepare yourself, be professional and well informed. Once again, you are out there *and will be judged*, and so will your work.

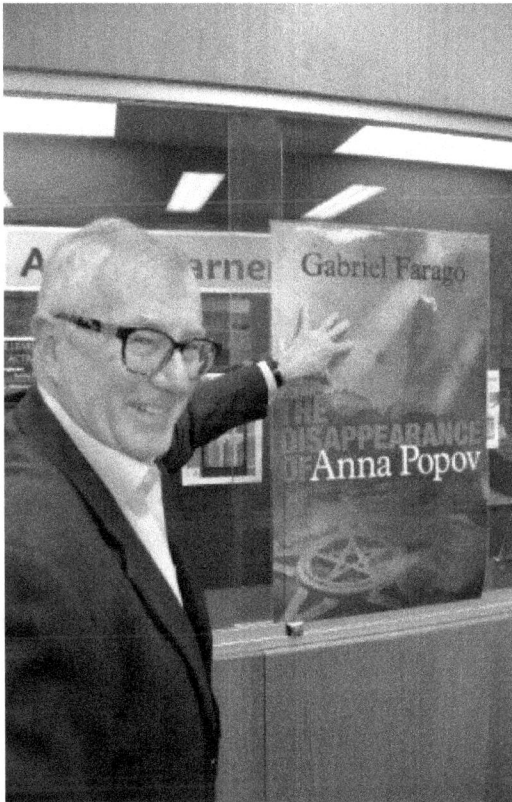

However, a word of caution is needed here. Unless you are confident that you can do this well and your delivery is polished, engaging and professional, it may be better to decline rather than embarrass yourself. Discuss this with your editor and friends. Have a trial run first and see how it goes. Don't rush in. Remember, reputations can take a lifetime to build, but can be destroyed in the blink of an eye!

I would once again like to pause here for a moment to make an important point. Many argue that social media campaigns, author platforms, book launches, talks and seminars and the like do not sell books. I beg to differ. In the current, ever-changing publishing environment everything appears to come down to one thing: *discoverability*. Please remember that word because I believe it will be the most important one you will take away with you from this little exercise.

'And what exactly does this mean?'

Here, let me tell you.

Discoverability

So far, we've considered a few 'little gems' which have a bearing on self-publishing. It's now time to hold up the jewel in the crown: *discoverability*. However, as you'll soon find out, everything is interrelated.

Most, if not all of your book sales, both in ebook format and in print, will be generated through the internet. That's an inescapable fact. Once you realise this, you will also understand that you are competing with tens of thousands of books in an unforgiving market. Your book is one little pebble on a huge beach littered with thousands. So, what will make someone notice your pebble and pick it up? What will make it stand out? That's the challenge, and it all comes down to *discoverability*. In short, potential readers have to *notice* you, and must be able to *find* you. Everything we've spoken about in Part II so far, comes down to this in the end. Therefore, there isn't one single thing that will do all that. *Everything* is interrelated, and acts together in concert.

Once you have a reputation and you've become a *name*, perhaps even a celebrity, people will find you; easily. But for now, you aren't there, just yet, and you have to fight your way through the publishing jungle and climb that mountain, and discoverability will be that all-important rope-ladder that will help you get to the top.

Much has been written about this, and no doubt you'll find many helpful publications on the subject. However, I would like to refer you to just one, namely, *How I Sold 1 Million eBooks in 5 Months*, by John Locke, available now on www.amazon.com.au.

A FINAL WORD

My final message to you is simple: *it can be done!* I sincerely hope that the few thoughts, suggestions and ideas I wanted to share with you have been of some value. The aim of this little book was certainly not to confuse you with technical detail and perhaps overwhelm you with too many challenges and thus deter you from attempting to climb that daunting mountain. It doesn't contain all the answers, nor does it profess to be a self-publishing manual telling you how you should do things. I merely wanted to share my little self-publishing journey with you and encourage you to have a go by showing you what I've done, what's worked for me, and why.

To be able to share your thoughts and ideas with others is not only exciting, it is a privilege which, due to the extraordinary changes in the publishing world, has become accessible to just about everyone prepared to have a go. This is every author's dream, and I'm sure it's yours, too.

So, keep polishing your work until it shines and you are satisfied that it is as good as you can make it. Then put on your climbing gear, get out your map, engage a competent guide and begin to tackle that mountain. I promise you, if you are prepared to do all that, you will be surprised how quickly you will step out of the woods, rise above the clouds and see that sparkling summit beckoning ahead. And before you know it, you will overcome all the obstacles and challenges standing in your way, and reach the top.

There are no words to describe how that will feel. Suffice it to say that you will experience a tremendous sense of achievement and satisfaction as you look down on the path you've travelled, and what you've accomplished along the way. It is my genuine hope that you will be able to experience all that, and nothing could give me greater pleasure than to know that this little book has in a small way contributed to your success.

Gabriel Farago

Further reading

It would have been very easy to overwhelm you with reference material here. However, I believe that would have been a mistake. Why? Because too much information can be confusing and therefore counterproductive, and that would most certainly have been the case here.

Consequently, I've decided to refer you to just one inexpensive, accessible and easy to follow publication available on Amazon which I've found most useful, and which I'm sure you will, too. In fact, I've already referred to it in the text. You can download it right now, and if you haven't already done so, may I suggest that you do so now because it will complement what we've talked about.

The book has been written by a highly successful author and his contribution based on firsthand experience in our subject matter will, in my view, be most helpful and valuable to you.

How I Sold 1 Million eBooks in 5 Months!

by John Locke

Available from Amazon:
http://www.amazon.com//dp/B0056BMK6K/

www.ingramcontent.com/pod-product-compliance
Lightning Source LLC
Chambersburg PA
CBHW072155020426
42334CB00018B/2016